Samuel Williston, William Seymour Tyler

A Discourse Commemorative of Honourable Samuel Williston

Samuel Williston, William Seymour Tyler

A Discourse Commemorative of Honourable Samuel Williston

ISBN/EAN: 9783337817732

Printed in Europe, USA, Canada, Australia, Japan

Cover: Foto ©Thomas Meinert / pixelio.de

More available books at **www.hansebooks.com**

A DISCOURSE

COMMEMORATIVE OF

HON. SAMUEL WILLISTON,

DELIVERED IN THE

PAYSON CHURCH AT EASTHAMPTON,

SEPTEMBER 13, 1874,

AND ALSO IN

THE COLLEGE CHURCH AT AMHERST, SEPTEMBER 20.

BY W. S. TYLER,

WILLISTON PROFESSOR OF GREEK IN AMHERST COLLEGE.

CLARK W. BRYAN AND COMPANY, PRINTERS.
1874.

DISCOURSE.

As we gather in this sacred place and come under the shadow of this solemn occasion, the very air we breathe seems to be full of voices. And it is not the noise and tumult of the world—it is not the speech of men or of angels—it is the voice of God that speaks to us. And as we listen and strive to hear and learn what He would say unto us, I seem to hear, uttered as distinctly almost as with an audible voice, such words as these : God only is great; God only is wise; there is none good but one, that is God. All flesh is as grass, and all the glory of man as the flower of grass. The grass withereth, and the flower thereof falleth away ; but the word of the Lord endureth forever. Let not the wise man glory in his wisdom, neither let the mighty man glory in his might; let not the rich man glory in his riches, but let him that glorieth, glory in this, that he understandeth and knoweth me ; that I am the Lord which exercise loving-kindness, judgment and righteousness, in the earth. The righteous shall flourish like the palm tree; he shall grow like a cedar in Lebanon. Those that be planted in the house of the Lord, shall flourish in the courts of our God. Blessed is the man that feareth the Lord; that delighteth greatly in his commandments. Wealth and riches shall be in his house, and his righteousness endureth forever. A good man showeth favor, and lendeth; he will guide his affairs with discretion. He hath dispersed; he hath given to the poor; his righteousness endureth forever; his horn shall be exalted with honor. There is that scattereth, and yet increaseth; and there is that withholdeth more than is meet, but it tendeth to poverty. The liberal soul shall be made fat, and he that watereth, shall be watered also himself. Give, and it shall be given unto you; good measure, pressed down and shaken together and running over, shall men give into your bosom. For with the same measure that ye mete withal, it shall be measured to you again. It is required in stewards that a man be found faithful. Who then is that faithful and wise steward, whom his lord shall make ruler over his household. Blessed is that servant whom his lord, when he cometh, shall find

so doing. Of a truth, I say unto you, he will
make him ruler over all that he hath. Blessed are
ye that sow beside all waters. Cast thy bread
upon the waters, for thou shalt find it after many
days. If thou draw out thy soul to the hungry,
and satisfy the afflicted soul; then shall thy light
rise in obscurity and thy darkness be as the noon-
day. And the Lord shall guide thee continually and
satisfy thy soul in drought, and make fat thy
bones: and thou shalt be like a watered garden
and like a spring of water whose waters fail not.
And they that be of thee shall build the old waste
places; thou shalt raise up the foundations of
many generations; and thou shalt be called, The
Repairer of the breach, The Restorer of paths to
dwell in.

All these Scriptures are naturally suggested by
the occasion which has called us together. They
are all more or less strikingly illustrated in the
life, or impressed upon us by the death of our
departed friend. God who, at sundry times, and
in divers manners, wrote them in His word, now
repeats them, as it were, in our ears by His Providence. May He also, by His Spirit, write them
in our hearts. Either of them might furnish a
suitable and profitable theme for our special medi-

tation at this hour. Each of them has occurred
in rapid succession as a proper text for this discourse. But none of them, perhaps, expresses in
so few and fitting words the characteristic life-work
of Samuel Williston—the mission which he seems
to have been sent into the world to accomplish—as
a part of the last passage which I have read. It
is found in the fifty-eighth chapter of Isaiah, and
the twelfth verse.

" *Thou shall raise up the foundations of many generations ; and thou shall be called, The Repairer of
the breach, The Restorer of paths to dwell in.*" Isa.
lviii. 12.

And the lesson which the providence and the
word of God commend to our especial consideration at this time is, The honor which is due to the
founders of institutions, especially institutions of
education and religion, for the benefit of many
generations.

The honor which is due to such men is seen,

1. In the high estimation in which they have
always been held, both by God and by mankind.

The two names, most honored of God in the history of the church and the world, are Moses and
Christ. And these are the names of the *founders*
and *lawgivers* of the Jewish and the Christian church.

Next in honor to Moses in the Old Testament,
stand David and Solomon, of whom the one planned
and the other built the temple, and both instituted
the worship of the Sanctuary—both organized the
outward kingdom of God on earth, with its palace
on the literal Mount Zion, and its capital the
earthly Jerusalem. The most illustrious of all the
followers of Christ was Paul, the founder of so
large a part of the Apostolic churches. And while
these men have been so highly honored of God,
what names have been so widely known or so
highly exalted as these, among men? Who of all
that have ever lived on earth, can compare with
them in the extent, the power or the sacredness
of their influence?

In profane history, again, what names have been
so honored in all ages and nations, as the founders of states, of schools, and of religious institutions. "The true marshalling of the degrees of
sovereign honors," says Lord Bacon, "are these:
In the first place are Conditores, *founders* of states.
In the second place, are Legislatores, lawgivers,
which are sometimes called second founders, or
Perpetui Principes, because they govern by their
ordinances after they are gone." Then follow in
regular gradation downwards, in the third place,

liberators; in the fourth, military defenders; and
last, civil rulers, all of whom the great philosopher
ranks below founders and lawgivers. Orpheus,
Amphion and Epimenides, among the founders of
religious rites and mysteries; Minos, Lycurgus and
Solon, among the founders of states; and Socrates,
Plato and Aristotle, among the founders of schools,
must suffice as illustrious examples from ancient
history. For the time would fail us to tell of Zo-
roaster and Confucius, of Boodha and Brahma, of
Romulus and Numa, and the other teachers, lawgivers and institution-founders of antiquity, who
lived at so early an age, that the imagination of
men has almost clothed them with the attributes
of gods. Still less can we enumerate the lesser
lights that organized governments, inaugurated re-
ligions and founded schools, and so extended their
influence and perpetuated their memory in the
later periods. In Mediæval and Modern history,
what greater names are there than those of Alfred
the Great and Charlemagne, Washington and Jef-
ferson; and these are the names of founders at
once of states and schools, of nations and colleges,
of empires and universities. Such men as Clement
and Origen, the founders and teachers of the far-
famed school of Christian learning at Alexandria,

and of the other catechetical schools and theological seminaries of the early church, were among the chief of the early Christian Fathers. There are no names more hallowed in the Catholic church than the founders of those monasteries which, with all their sins, have the merit of keeping learning and religion alive through the darkness and confusion of the Middle Ages. The founders, too, of those religious orders whose influence has been felt to the remotest bounds of Christendom, what veneration is felt for them by all good Catholics, from age to age. The names of St. Benedict, St. Dominic, St. Francis, and Ignatius Loyola, have been canonized and embalmed in the religious societies which they established. And the founders of sects and of charitable and benevolent associations are scarcely less honored and revered among Protestants. The founders of the libraries, the scholarships and fellowships, and the separate colleges at Oxford and Cambridge, still live in those universities; their portraits and statues occupy the most conspicuous places in the halls, colleges and libraries which they established, and their names are still spoken with pride and pleasure, as they have been for centuries, by the noble youth who enjoy the benefit of their liberality. The greatest and best of

2

England's kings have been proud to identify their memories with these foundations. The good Queen Philippa founded Queen's College, and the queens of England have ever since been, *ex officio*, its patronesses. Christ Church College is the proudest monument of the proud Cardinal Wolsey—it might well be said to be his *only* enduring monument; and the other colleges bear up the names, otherwise little remembered and seldom spoken, of some of the chief dignitaries of the church and the state. Who has not heard the names of Bodley and Radcliff? They are the synonyms of libraries and books, wherever there are scholars.

In our own age and country, there is no surer passport to immortal remembrance than to be identified with the origin and progress of those institutions of learning, charity and religion which are the characteristic and chief glory of our times. Here specification is needless; for it were but to enumerate the principal academies, colleges and professional seminaries of New England—the chief charitable and religious as well as literary and scientific foundations of the country, so many of which hallow and perpetuate the names of their founders. Who can ever think of American missions without being reminded of Worcester and Evarts? It is

honor enough for any man to have had anything
to do with originating the Home Missionary, Tract,
Bible, Temperance and Anti-Slavery Societies. What
American scholar, aye, and what American citizen
has not often repeated the names of Harvard and
Yale? What educated man, nay, what intelligent
man, woman or child in the future periods of our
history will not be familiar with the names of Phillips
and Williston?

The honor which is due to the founders of institutions, especially those of learning and religion,
may be seen

2. In the nature and value of these institutions.

An institution is the embodiment of a principle,
the organization and thus the multiplication and extension of a power, the incarnation and perpetua-
tion of a life. Sparta was a perpetuated Lycurgus
Athens was Solon embodied and endowed with a
kind of immortality. The Christian Church is the
body of Christ—is Christ living, suffering, dying,
rising again from age to age, and thus at length
triumphing and reigning on earth as in heaven.
A hospital with its succession of physicians and
nurses, a charitable society with its successive corps
of officers and agents and its undying ministries to

the poor, the sick and the suffering, is a perpetual metempsychosis of Howard the philanthropist; only it is a larger, richer, mightier Howard better trained and better furnished for his work—the soul of Howard animating the body of a hundred-headed and hundred-handed giant, and employing all its heads and all its hands in agencies of beneficence, and that giant perchance vested not only with ubiquity but with immortality. A school well endowed, and so sustained from generation to generation, is a school-master that never dies. Rugby is Arnold teaching and ruling in the hearts of his pupils long after Arnold is dead. Phillips has ceased from his labors, and his personal influence can no longer be traced. Phillips Academy not only prolongs but multiplies his labors, not only perpetuates but enlarges his influence, not only transmits his wealth but transmutes it into the fine gold of a classical and Christian education. For while institutions are incarnations of ideas and principles, they may be, and frequently are, spiritualizations of material forces, transfigurations of gross earthly substances into something quite ethereal and divine. An institution, like a manufacturing establishment, can put in motion many hands instead of one or two, and those of far more delicacy and dexterity than the

fingers of the founder. An institution can perpetuate the name and the influence of the intelligent
and excellent, but perhaps uneducated and person-
ally uninfluential manufacturer or merchant, in a
corps of elegant scholars and able teachers that will
fashion the minds, the morals and the manners of
scores, perhaps hundreds of youth in every generation till the end of time. Institutions, like skillful
enginery, employ natural agencies, subsidize auxiliary forces, and enlist powers and resources that
are more than human.

Institutions educate and control individual men.
They also fashion society, guide the church and
govern the nation. Institutions mark and make
civilization. Savages *have* no institutions, just as
they have no machines. Just in proportion as civilization advances, institutions become more numerous and complicated, more elevated and refined.
Every step of *Christian* civilization is marked and
maintained, and in no small measure made by Christian schools, colleges, seminaries of learning, and
institutions of charity and benevolence. Institutions
mark and make progress. They link the past with
the present, and the present with the future. They
constitute an open channel of communication—nay,
a vital union and communion between the ages.

They enrich each generation with the wisdom and virtue of previous generations, and make the acquisitions and resources of individuals the wealth and power of the state, the age and the race.

All these remarks, while they are true of institutions in general, apply with emphasis to institutions of learning, especially when sanctified by religion. These are emphatically the great conservative and progressive, civilizing and educating, perpetuating and transfiguring powers of society; the living channels of communication between the Ancient and the Modern, the Old World and the New, the individual and his age and race. They transmute the gold and silver and houses and lands of the founder into the true riches of the mind and heart, and then transmit them through the ages and nations, thus enduing them with something like ubiquity and immortality. They live on, though founders and teachers die, and even after states and nations have passed away; as a tree lives on, though its leaves fall from year · to year, — lives when planters and owners, one after another, pass away, and not unfrequently still lives when the nation and race that planted it and long ate its fruit, have given place to others. "Aye be planting a tree," was a precept of Scotch wisdom—if I mis-

take not, it was addressed to Jeanie Deans by her
father in the Heart of Mid Lothian. "Aye be
planting a tree, Jeanie; it will be growing when
you are asleep, it will live when you are dead.
Those who come after you will sit under its shade
and eat of its fruit." So an institution of learning
and religion will still be growing and working
when its founder has ceased to toil or care for it
—will live long after he is laid in the grave; it
will bear fruit at all seasons of the year and pro-
duce all manner of fruit, while, peradventure, its
very leaves will be for the healing of the nations.
Thus the libraries and museums at Alexandria
survived dynasties and outlived the Grecian and
Roman supremacy, educating all the while Jews
and Greeks, Asiatics, Africans and Europeans,
mediating between philosophy and revelation, and
propagating learning and religion together among
the leading minds of three continents. The schools
of the Byzantine grammarians formed the con-
necting link between the Ancient and the Modern civilizations, as Constantinople itself is the
bridge between the East and the West; and by pre-
serving the wisdom of the Ancients, they gave rise
to the revival of learning in Modern Europe. Even
the monasteries, with their libraries, kept alive the

flickering torch of learning during the Dark Ages,
and thus helped to introduce the Reformation. For
while institutions of learning are the conservators
of the Old, they are no less emphatically the orig-
inators of the New. The revival of learning and
the reformation were both born and nurtured in
the Universities. The earliest and greatest of the
Reformers were monks and professors.

But it is, above all, the office of institutions of
learning to *educate :* to educate individuals and thus
to mould and fashion society; to educate the members, and especially the officers of the church, and
so to shape the character and history of the church
itself; to educate the citizens, and especially the
rulers of the State, and so to govern the State
and the Nation. They lay the *foundations* of society, government and religion. They are truly,
what they are often called, *Seminaries,* that is, they
sow the *seeds* of ideas and principles; they shape
and train the *germs* of private and public life and ac-
tion; they bend the *twig* of individual and national
character. The higher seminaries educate the leading minds, and thus teach and rule the masses.
They improve and perfect agriculture, commerce,
and all the useful arts by developing the sciences on
which they are founded. They purify the streams

of political, social, moral and religious life, by purify-
ing the fountain. Christian colleges and seminaries
formed the character of New England in the forming
period of her history, and New England, through
her own schools and colleges, and those which she
is founding all over the land, is ruling the church and
governing the nation. New England, through her
own colleges and seminaries, and those which she is
setting up like light-houses on foreign shores, is
carrying on the missionary work, and laying the
foundations of society and government, education
and religion for " many generations" in every part
of the world.

The honor which is due to the founders of institutions, especially those of learning and religion,
may be seen
3. In the broad views, high aims, and rare wisdom and excellence of character by which such
men must be distinguished.

The founders of *states* and nations, the authors
of constitutions, codes of law, and forms of government, are, of course, few; for few have either
the opportunity or the capacity to inaugurate such
institutions. It is not strange, therefore, that these
few should have been honored in all ages as the
3

special favorites both of earth and heaven. The
same is true also of the founders of new rites and
forms, sects and creeds in religion. But there is
almost unlimited opportunity to found churches,
schools, and all the various institutions of education and religion, where they do not exist, or exist
only in a very imperfect form. And there are
more in our day than there ever were before, perhaps, who prize and improve their privilege in
this respect. But they are still few in comparison with the many who do not attain, or even
aspire to it — very few, in comparison with the
many, many wants of a growing country, an ad-
vancing church and a perishing world. And the
reason is obvious. It requires rare disinterested-
ness, and rare discernment. Few men have the
self-denial and self-sacrifice, and perhaps fewer still
the insight and the foresight, the far-seeing sagac-
ity, and the far-reaching wisdom, which must be-
long to the founders of such institutions. Most
men are absorbed in themselves or their families,
their relatives and friends. If they do not spend
all their energies and resources in looking out for
themselves and their immediate connections, their
own church, their own party, or, at the very largest,
their own country is the extreme limit of their

vision. At all events, there must be something local, sectional, partial, exclusive, about an object that appeals to them, or it has no charms for them; and the more narrow and exclusive it is, the more attractive it will be to nine-tenths of mankind.

Most men are absorbed in the present. They never think of coming generations and future ages. They demand immediate results, quick returns, speedy harvests. Comparatively few will plant an orchard, or a single tree even, of which they cannot expect themselves to gather the fruit—still fewer a forest for the benefit of they know not what future generation. Few are capable of discerning the oak in the acorn, and very few have the patience to plant the acorn and watch and wait for its slow development.

Most men look only on the outward appearance, and can see only what is present and apparent to the senses. Of charitable men, the great majority would rather contribute for the supply of the wants of the body, than to the education of the immortal spirit, and prefer to meet the existing and perpetually recurring necessities of the poor rather than to seek ways and provide means for removing the causes of poverty. Nations built prisons long ages before they established schools; and to this day

nations and individuals are slower to endow colleges, than they are to found almshouses and hos-
pitals. It is only a few men of rare discernment—

>Souls destined to o'erleap the vulgar lot,
>And mould the world unto the scheme of God—

it is only such, who can pierce through the outward phenomena to the inward and spiritual causes,
who can look beyond immediate and temporary
issues to remote and permanent results; who are
willing to plant seeds for others to gather the fruit;
who, in short, and in the language of our text, have
the wisdom and the power to "raise up the foundations for many generations." It is, therefore, simple
even-handed justice to bestow rare honor on men
of such rare wisdom and virtue; to perpetuate their
memories by making them commensurate with the
duration of the institutions which they have founded;
to mete out to them a height of renown, a breadth
of esteem and a depth of veneration corresponding
with the breadth and length and height and depth
of their foundations, and the comprehensiveness of
views and elevation of sentiments by which they
were distinguished: it is right and proper that
those who have studied and labored and prayed
and denied themselves, and sacrificed themselves to

educate and enrich the minds and hearts of many generations, should be enshrined in the grateful and affectionate remembrance of men from age to age.

On this principle, few will receive higher honor than the founders of Christian colleges and seminaries of learning. And among the founders of such institutions, few in this or in other lands, in ancient or in modern times, deserve a higher place in public estimation, than Samuel Williston.

The community generally, and especially the numerous youth who have enjoyed the benefits of his wisdom and munificence, will desire to know something of the early life and history of a man who has been so successful in business and made such an exemplary use of his large acquisitions.

Samuel Williston was born in Easthampton, June 17, 1795. Thus his birthday was the twentieth anniversary of the Battle of Bunker Hill. He was the son of Rev. Payson Williston, of Easthampton, who was the son of Rev. Noah Williston, of West Haven, Conn., who had four children, two sons, both of whom were ministers, and two daughters, both of whom were ministers' wives. On his father's side he was own cousin to Rev. Richard Salter

Storrs, D. D., of Braintree, and so akin, not only
to the Willistons and Storrses, but to the Paysons,
the Strongs, the Elys and the other illustrious clergy-
men whose names Professor Park has recently woven
like a garland about the brow of the Braintree
pastor. His mother, Mrs. Sarah Birdseye Williston,
was also the daughter of a Connecticut clergyman,
Rev. Nathan Birdseye, of Stratford.

His parents and grandparents were all remarkable for their longevity. His father lived to the
age of 93, and *his* father to the age of 77; his
mother to the age of 82, and *her* father to his 103d
year—all thus exceeding the appointed limit of
threescore years and ten, and all doubtless exem-
plifying the fifth commandment, which Paul calls
the first commandment with promise: "Honor thy
father and thy mother, that thy days may be long
upon the land which the Lord thy God giveth thee."
Mr. Williston himself had almost reached the age
of fourscore years; and yet with the humble piety
of the patriarch of Israel he could and would have
said: "Few and evil have the days of the years of
my life been, and have not attained unto the days
of the years of the life of my fathers in the days
of their pilgrimage."

His father will be remembered by some of this

audience, as he is well remembered by the speaker,
as one of the gentlest, kindest, loveliest men that
ever walked the earth, too modest to know his
own worth, too meek sometimes to assert his own
rights, almost too honest, unsuspecting, unselfish and
unworldly to live in such a world as this; not a
great man but, as every body would say, a good
man; not an eloquent preacher, but his life a perpetual and most eloquent sermon on the golden
rule, and his very face beaming with cheerfulness
and benignity on all around him. No wonder he
lived to be almost a hundred years old. I only
wonder that such a man should die at all; and
when I returned from Europe and was told that
the good old man was gone, it seemed to me that
he must have been translated. Father Williston's
salary never amounted to $300. He had, however,
a settlement of £70, with which he bought a small
farm of thirty-three acres of poor land, whereon he
used to work in haying time and a few hours a
day at other seasons, to eke out a scanty subsist-
ence for his family.

Mrs. Williston, Samuel's mother, was born to be
a helpmeet to such a poor minister. This excellent
couple possessed, as husband and wife always should
possess, the qualities and habits that are mutually

compensative the one to the other, so as together
to make a perfect whole. She was as industrious
and faithful in the parsonage as he was in the par-
ish; as economical as he was liberal; as careful and
anxious as he was cheerful and happy; a very Martha
for household care and thrift, though not without
Mary's part also in the one thing needful. While
he united in himself many of the characteristics of
both his parents, Samuel bore a striking resemblance
in person, mind and manners to his mother. Bound
by the customs of the age to exercise hospitality
as well as to provide things honest in the sight of
all men, I have heard her say that she often had
some ministerial brother, with his whole family, stop
for dinner, or perchance to stay over night, when
there was not enough in the whole house to give
them a single meal. Yet the dinner was always
forthcoming, the table comfortable and the whole
house in perfect order. The barrel of meal was
never quite empty, and the cruse of oil never failed.
Thus patient industry and strict economy were beau-
tifully wedded to generous hospitality and Christian
liberality in the household of the first pastor of
Easthampton, as they always joined hand in hand
and walked side by side in the life of his distinguished son.

A family of six children were born in that parsonage, and all but one (who died in childhood) were brought up and educated on that salary, with the help which they were taught to render to themselves and their parents—brought up to habits of industry and economy, and educated in the principles of virtue and piety; and now there is wealth enough in the family to cover every inch of that poor farm over with dollars. Of his two brothers, one was Dea. J. P. Williston of Northampton, the reformer and philanthropist, whose humane and Christian charities, beginning at home, compassed the globe, dropping like the rain and distilling like the dew on the dry and thirsty land. The other, Dea. N. B. Williston, president of a bank in Brattleboro, Vt., a man of like spirit with his brothers, is the only surviving member of the family. Of his two sisters, one was the wife of J. D. Whitney, Esq., of Northampton, and the mother of the distinguished professors of that name; the other was the mother of the late Mrs. Dr. Adams of Boston.

Samuel, though the third child that was born to his parents, was the oldest son that grew up to manhood. The trials and triumphs of his education and his early business, and the story of his marriage, constitute a romance in real life of rare interest

4

and pathos. He began to go to school very young, and attended the district school in his native place, summer and winter, till he was ten years old; then in the winter only till he was sixteen, at which age his *schooling*, as it was called, that is, his instruction in the common school, which then scarcely extended beyond reading, writing and the rudiments of arithmetic, ceased altogether. He began to work on a farm at the early age of ten, in the absence of his father on a missionary tour of three months in the State of New York. This first work was done on the farm, and under the direction of a good deacon in his father's church, Dea. Solomon Lyman, whose memory he always held in high esteem and veneration. After this he worked on a farm every summer till he was sixteen, sometimes on his father's, sometimes for some of his parishioners, and the last of these summers out of town in Westhampton, where his wages were $7 a month. These facts in his early life are not only of interest by way of contrast with his subsequent prosperity, but he was wont to attach great importance to these early labors as training him to habits of industry, and still more as laying the foundations of that bodily health and strength without which he was persuaded he never could have accomplished his life-work.

After he ceased going to school, he studied to
some extent privately with his father, though
only in the winter, for he was obliged to work
in the summer. He loved study and longed for
a liberal education. But he saw no way, in which
he could obtain the requisite means. He therefore went into a clothier's shop belonging to a
brother-in-law in Rochester, Vt., where he labored the greater part of two winters, till he
became master of the art to such an extent
that he was entrusted with the charge of the
shop. Meanwhile he lost no time, spent his even-
ings in reading, and made the most of all the
means of self-education within his reach. His desire for a better education being thus increased,
on his return from Vermont, late in the winter
of 1813–14, he entered Westfield Academy. But
his funds were exhausted before he had com-
pleted a single term, and he came home again
to study with his father. Still encouraged by
his teachers and his parents, that where there was
a will there was a way, and that some way would be
found for him yet to go through college, he now
began to study Latin, which he pursued first with
his father and then with Rev. Mr. Gould, of
Southampton. In the summer of 1814, learning

that there were funds at Andover for the aid of
indigent students, and attracted by the excellence
of the institution, he went to Phillips Academy,
then under the principal charge of Rev. John
Adams, and enjoying the instructions also of Mr.
Hawes, afterwards Dr. Hawes, of the Centre Church
in Hartford, Conn. It took more time and more
money then to go to Andover than it does now.
Young Williston could not afford to go by stage,
then the only public conveyance. His father
therefore carried him one day's ride to Brookfield,
where, according to the hospitable and ministerial usages of the times, they lodged at the house
of the pastor. The next day he walked to
Worcester. Fatigue then compelled him to ride
to Boston. From Boston he set out on foot again
for Andover, but caught a ride a part of the way
on a farmer's wagon. He had no trunk, no valise
or carpet-bag; all he had with him, pretty much
everything he had in the world, was tied up in a
bundle. At Andover, for the sake of economy,
though not disliking the long walk for its own
sake and for exercise, he boarded a mile and a half
from the Academy. Yet he was never tardy. He
never failed in a recitation. He went there to do
his best. He always did do the best that he could.

He obeyed all the rules of the school. He ex-
celled in his studies. He went up at a step from
the Epitome of Sacred History over the class in
Viri Romae to the class in Selectae a Sacris et
Profanis, and on examination at the close of his
first term, he was placed upon the foundation as
a charity scholar. Now he had reached a point
from which he thought he could see the goal of
his ambition, a college education. Now he was
satisfied and regarded his fortune as made, or at
least quite secure. But severer trials awaited him.
He had not been there a year when his eye-sight
failed him. and he was obliged to leave. For two
years, now, from the spring of 1815 to that of
1817, he vibrated between labor on the farm and
a clerkship in a store, passing the larger part of
the time in the store, but with intervals of two
or three months on the farm, suffering all the
while from weakness, inflammation and incessant
pain in the eyes, till at length he gave up all
hope of being or doing anything that could satisfy his ambition. He made up his mind—this
is the way in which he was in the habit of speaking
of it—that he must be a farmer, and a poor man
at that. These years, however, were by no means
lost to him. In the store of Justin Ely of West

Springfield, and still more in the large wholesale
establishment of Francis Child of New York city,
with whom he spent a year, he was acquiring that
knowledge of men and things, and forming those
ideas and habits of business which were afterwards to be of such essential service to him in
the management of his own affairs. Moreover it
was during this period, under the discipline of repeated disappointments and sore trials, accompanied by the effectual teaching of the Holy Spirit,
that he began life anew as a Christian, and after
a severe inward struggle, which began soon after
leaving Andover and ended in submission and peace
just before going to New York, he consecrated
himself publicly to the service of God as a member of the Presbyterian church under the pastoral
care of Rev. Dr. Spring.

In the spring of 1817, at the age of 22, baffled
in all his plans by the failure of his eyes, and
almost disheartened by the double disappointment
consequent upon it, first in regard to a college
education, and then in his experiments in the mercantile line, he came back to his father and pro-
posed to him to go into the farming business; the
father to furnish the farm and the capital, and the
son to manage it and do the work. The father

reluctantly consented, invested some four or five
hundred dollars from *his* father's estate, in the
purchase of land, taking the deed of it in his own
name, and then borrowed money for the purchase
of more land and implements of husbandry. Thus
unpromising was the commencement of Mr. Williston's business life, without capital, almost without
anything that he could call his own, and having
run his father in debt for the very tools with
which he was to do his work. He continued to
follow farming as his business four years, enlarging
the farm and extending the business, varying it
also by raising sheep and growing fine wool, till he
became, for that place and those times, quite a
large farmer and wool-grower. He worked on the
farm himself, however, only in the summer. In
the winter, he betook himself to that unfailing re-
source of intelligent and aspiring youth of both
sexes in Yankee land, teaching school. The first
winter, he taught in the North district in Easthampton, for $16 a month, boarding himself and
walking more than a mile to and from school, and
doing all the chores at home, morning and evening.
The next year, he taught the large scholars in the
Center district at Southampton, taking, in the
spring, the place which had been filled by a col-

lege student in the winter. The following winter,
he taught five months in Northampton. He next
taught, in the years 1820–21, for fourteen months
consecutively, the grammar school in Springfield,
at the same time *managing* the farm and carrying
on the work with hired help, and the aid of his
younger brothers. During the winter of 1821–22,
he taught a select school in Easthampton.

In the spring of 1822, (May 27,) he was married
to Miss Emily Graves, daughter of Elnathan Graves,
a respectable farmer, in moderate circumstances, in
the neighboring town of Williamsburg. They had
been engaged three years previous, the marriage
being delayed from economical and prudential con-
siderations. Partly to illustrate the simplicity of
the times, and partly to show his own limited
means, I have heard him say that he was married
in a coat which he had worn two years for Sun-
days and holidays, and that they took no bridal
tour or excursion after the marriage. Or, to tell
the story more exactly, their only bridal excursion
was to Rum Brook, at the foot of Mount Tom, in
Easthampton, where they had a bottle of wine and
some plain cake for their entertainment. Almost
half a century afterwards, happening to call upon
them on the forty-eighth anniversary of their mar-

riage, I found them preparing to celebrate it at the same place in the same beautiful and simple way. Are the brides and grooms of our day, who think they must cross the ocean, or mayhap go round the world for their bridal tour—are they wiser or happier than this worthy couple? He brought his wife home to the house of his father, and the two families lived together under the same roof in beautiful harmony and mutual love for twenty-one years, only enlarging the old parsonage and beautifying the grounds to correspond with the growth of business and their increasing prosperity.

He still taught one year, after being married, in the Central district school in Easthampton, thus making five winters in all, besides the entire year of his teaching in Springfield. Meanwhile the farming business went on, enlarging, as we have said, and on the whole prospering. But he was obliged to run in debt at the outset. This debt was still further increased for the sake of enlarging the business. He had invested in land and sheep, $1,800, most of which was borrowed capital. His first crop of wool was lost through the failure of the purchaser. Two or three hundred dollars a year was all that could be saved for repairing this

5

loss and reducing this burden of indebtedness. Mrs. Williston has remarked, that at this time it was a daily subject of prayer at the domestic altar that God would open to him ways and means by which he might obtain a competence for himself and family. And now, at length—doubtless in answer to those very prayers, and as the result too of the severe discipline to which he had been subjected—the way was to be opened. And the relief was to come through the wife whom God had given him to be not only his companion and helpmeet in general, but his wise counselor and his good genius in that very thing which he had so often made a subject of special prayer. Mrs. Williston had never felt able to keep the help she needed in housekeeping, nor to give what she wished in aid of charitable objects. While looking about for relief and enlargement in these particulars, she found that her mother had been in the habit of making covered buttons for her own family, and a small surplus for sale to others. She took up the business at once on a somewhat larger scale. The first package of buttons which she made, she took to Mr. David Whitney, of Northampton, (long the Treasurer of the Hampshire County Missionary Society,) as a contribution of the first-fruits to the cause of missions; and President Humphrey, happening in about that time, became the first purchaser. Little did he or she think, that there was the germ of Williston Seminary and Williston College.

A button machine ought to be graven on the seal of one, if not both of these institutions; and the founders should be represented by a double bust of Mr. and Mrs. Williston, not set back to back like some of the old Greek sculptures, but putting their heads and hands together in the manufacture of covered buttons. Then if Christian art could in some way represent the work of missions and the kingdom and glory of God in full view before their eyes, illumining their pathway, irradiating their persons, and making their upturned faces shine with the light of heaven, the picture would be quite complete.

But to return to our narrative. The second package was sent to Arthur Tappan, of New York, who immediately contracted for twenty-five gross at two dollars a gross. Fifty dollars! Never in all their subsequent wealth did they feel so rich as when they received that order from the firm of Arthur Tappan. The first buttons Mrs. Williston made with her own hands. Then she employed other hands to work for

her in the house. Next she began to give out buttons to be made in neighboring families. Mr. Williston soon perceived that here was a field of enterprise
wider and more promising than farming, and that
instead of making her time and toil merely subsid-
iary to his work, he might better make his minister to hers. It was in 1826, when he was already
more than thirty years of age, that the beginning
was made of this new undertaking. In 1827, he
went to New York, found customers, received
orders, and went back to extend his business.
Soon he went in like manner to Philadelphia, Balti-
more and Boston, and established agencies in all the
principal cities of the United States. The business
grew rapidly, and it was only a short time, before he
had more than a thousand families at work making
buttons for him, through all that circle of towns,
thirty or forty miles in diameter, of which Easthampton was the center. Auxiliary to the button
business, he opened a store, and, for a number of
years, carried on quite a large business for the
country, in the sale of dry goods, his first clerk
being Mr. Knight, and Mrs. Williston his first book-
keeper.

The manufacture went on in this way by hand,
employing thousands of busy and skillful fingers

in a constantly extending circle of private families,
and rewarding their industry with a corresponding
increase of the comforts and elegancies of life,
for ten or a dozen years, when Providence opened
the way for a still greater improvement and enlargement. In one of his visits to New York,
Mr. Williston found there some buttons of English
manufacture, made without thread, without needle,
I had almost said without fingers, in short, manifestly made by machinery. He took these buttons
to the Messrs. Joel and Josiah Hayden, who were
then just beginning to be known as ingenious and
enterprising mechanics in Williamsburg, and pro-
posed to furnish the capital, sell the goods and
divide the profits equally, if they would discover
the process, get up the machinery and manufacture the buttons. They entered with characteristic zeal and energy upon the experiment, and
worked on patiently with hands and brains for
years before their labors were crowned with
complete success. It was a full year before they
could make a button. When they had succeeded
to some extent, they derived great assistance from
a colored man who had been an employee in an
English factory and knew the machinery and the
process. Whether the memory of this timely ser-

vice was, in any measure, the cause of their life-long
friendship for the colored race, or whether Providence sent this man to serve them in return for
what it was already in their hearts to do for the
cause of humanity and to furnish them the means
for more enlarged philanthropy in coming years,
I do not know. But I can not but see in this
incident, as well as in the connection of Arthur
Tappan and President Humphrey with this enterprise, not only interesting coincidences, but illus-
trations of that almost poetical justice and fitness
which the Greeks were so fond of noting, and
which no close observer can fail to mark, sometimes at least, in the providence of God.

The perfecting of this machinery and the successful carrying on of the manufacture made the
fortunes of both parties. It was the making—
it was, at least, the beginning of Haydenville. It
has since done the same service to Easthampton.
Mr. Williston used often to speak of the perfect
harmony and happiness of his business relations
with Mr. Hayden—a harmony which was expressed and increased by their traveling in Europe
together, and at length still farther cemented by
a marriage connection between the families. This
harmonious co-operation continued without interrup-

tion, twelve years, till in 1847, by mutual consent, the partnership was dissolved, and, at once for the personal convenience of Mr. Williston and for the benefit of his native place, the button business was transferred to Easthampton.

We have dwelt on these earlier years of Mr. Williston's business life with a particularity which may perhaps require some apology. He was a business man, and it is as an able and successful business man that we wish to know his history. These earlier years of his life are unknown to the younger portion of the community, and have more or less faded from the memory of the older inhabitants. While they developed his character and formed his habits, they illustrate also the providence of God. While they set before us a remarkable example of patience and perseverance, of faith and hope in God, finally triumphing and rejoicing in the manifest blessing of heaven, they forcibly teach this great lesson, that we should never despise small things—that nothing is in reality small, since things apparently the smallest may lead to the greatest results.

It was when he was a little over forty that Mr. Williston began to lay "foundations" and build not only for himself but for his native town and for the larger public. In 1837 he bore a prominent part in the erection of the house of worship now occupied by the first church in Easthampton. In 1841 he established Williston Seminary. In 1843 he built his own house. Early in 1845 he founded the Williston Professorship of Rhetoric and Oratory in Amherst College. Later in the same year, he spent six months in traveling in Europe. In the winter of 1846-7 he founded the Graves Professorship, now the Williston Professorship of Greek, and one-half of the Hitchcock Professorship of Natural Theology and Geology in Amherst College, thus making in all the sum of $50,000, which he had already given for permanent foundations in that institution.

It was in 1847 that he removed his business from Haydenville to Easthampton. From that time to the present, we need not dwell on the details of his private life, for they are fresh in the memory of us all. I need not remind you how he went on adding factory to factory and one species of business to another, house to house, block to block, and even village to village, till from one of the smallest, Easthampton has become one of the largest and most populous towns in Hampshire county. I need not tell you how he has built churches,

and enlarged the grounds and multiplied the edifices of Williston Seminary, and increased the funds
and the faculty of the Seminary and of Amherst
College, and extended and diffused his donations for
public, charitable, educational and religious objects,
corresponding with the increase of his wealth and
the demands of the times, till his name has become
identified with all the great benevolent enterprises
of the age, and his influence is felt all over the
world.

Mr. Williston has filled not a few posts of honor
and trust. He was a member of the Lower House
of the Massachusetts Legislature in 1841, and a
member of the Senate in 1842 and 1843. He was
elected to the Legislature as an Anti-Slavery Whig,
and might doubtless have continued to occupy and
adorn public life, if he had not, after three years'
legislative service, declined a re-election. In politics, he has always been known as belonging to the
school of progress and reform. He was usually in
advance of his party and of the age, a full believer
in the doctrine of the *higher law,* and the applica-
tion of Christian ethics to the legislative, executive
and judiciary departments of the government, and
therefore sometimes charged with political heresy
and fanaticism, though he was never an impracti-

6

cable or an extremist. In the great struggle for
the integrity and existence of the nation, he was
ever among the firmest supporters of the government, and among the most strenuous advocates for
the extinction of slavery as the chief cause of all
our troubles. While a member of the Legislature,
,in 1841, he was chosen by that body a trustee of
Amherst College. For thirty-three years, the aver-
age duration of human life, and throughout one
entire generation, he has not only been a member
of the Corporation, but during the larger part of
these years a member also of the Prudential Committee and often of special committees on build-
ings and business matters of the utmost importance, and until the recent failure of his health he
was from principle an unfailing attendant of ordi-
nary and extraordinary meetings of the board, and
unsparing not only of his money, of which he gave
during his life a hundred and fifty thousand dollars
from time to time as it was wanted, and would do
the most good, but also of his time, which, for a
man of business and wealth, it is often far more diffi-
cult to give than money. For the same number of
years he has been not only trustee, but president
of the trustees of Williston Seminary, and with
only two exceptions, the one occasioned by sickness

and the other by absence from the country, he has
presided in all the meetings. He has been the acting treasurer also of the Seminary, and has watched
over all its external and internal affairs with the
same wise and careful personal supervision which
he has given to his business. Appointed by the
Governor and Council one of the first trustees of
the State Reform School, when that office was no
sinecure, he was of great service in erecting build-
ings, improving the farm and inaugurating the institution. He was one of the first trustees of Mount
Holyoke Seminary, of which he helped to lay the
foundations, and in which he ever felt a lively
interest. He was a corporate member of the American Board of Commissioners for Foreign Missions,
and for many years as constant in attendance on
its meetings as he was in contributions to its funds.

The business corporations, manufacturing com-
panies, banks, railways, gas and water power com-
panies in Easthampton, Northampton, Holyoke and
elsewhere, in which he was a leading corporator,
and usually president, are too numerous to men-
tion.

Mr. Williston's domestic life was marked by great
trials as well as great blessings, and had a most
important bearing on his character and history.   For

four years after their marriage, Mr. and Mrs. Williston lived without children. In 1831, they lost two children, then three and a half and one and a half years old, by scarlet fever. In 1837, they were called to experience the same deep affliction again in the loss, and by the same disease, of two children who had reached the age respectively of five and a half and three and a half. They were thus written childless twice in the space of six years, and have never since had children of their own. But they have adopted the children of missionaries and children who had been bereaved of their parents, whom they have reared and educated as their own; and few families, probably, have enjoyed more domestic happiness than theirs. And what is more, schools and churches and charitable societies without number have become their adopted children, have been nursed and cherished by them with a father's and a mother's love and made heirs to their inheritance. It was during the sickness of his last child that Mr. Williston, feeling that he had not done his whole duty as a steward of the Lord's property, consecrated himself anew to his service, set apart the principal and interest of a considerable investment for benevolent purposes, and thus entered on a new epoch in his Christian life.

The son and grandson of parents and grandparents, who were not only Christians but ministers
of the gospel, Mr. Williston early received the
most careful Christian culture and training. He
read the Bible through a great many times in his
childhood and youth—he usually read it through
every year. He was taught the Assembly's Cate-
chism, and not only said it from memory to his parents at home, but according to the usage of the times,
recited it in school every Saturday forenoon, and
repeated it from beginning to end, over and over
again in the church. He observed the Sabbath
with great strictness, and carefully avoided pro-
fanity and immorality of every kind. He not only
prayed in secret but led the family devotions at
his boarding-place in Andover, before he cherished
any hope of his personal interest in the salvation
by Christ. We might have expected such a young
man, so moral, upright and amiable, to enter upon
a religious life, without any great conflict or deep
conviction of sin. But this was far from being
the case. He was often much exercised about personal religion, but on his return from Andover,
disappointed in his hopes of education, and thwarted
in his plans for life, he passed through a severe
mental struggle, came under deep conviction of sin,

felt himself to be justly condemned by the law of
God, and, in himself, utterly ruined and undone;
and he continued in this state for months. It was
almost a year before he became clear in his belief
that he was a real Christian. There was no par-
ticular time to which he could point as the beginning of his religious life. Light and peace gradually
dawned upon his soul. Sudden and rapturous joy
was no part of his Christian experience. This
great event—for so he regarded it, though there was
nothing very marked about the time or the manner
of it—took place in 1816. Going to New York soon
after, he heard with great satisfaction, the preaching
of Dr. Romeyn, Dr. Mason and Dr. Spring, and in
the winter of 1816–17, he became a member of Dr.
Spring's church. When he left the city, he transferred his relation to the church under his father's
care in Easthampton, and in 1852 he went off with
others to form the Payson Church. He was for many
years a member of the committee, and a deacon in
the First Church, and in the Payson Church he held
both those offices from the beginning. He never
felt that he could serve God by proxy, however
numerous might be the agents whom he supported
in the Christian work; and munificent as his contributions were to the maintenance and propagation

of the gospel, he never thought or desired by this
to purchase any exemption from personal service.
At home and abroad, till the age of threescore
years and more, he rarely failed to attend three
services on the Sabbath, and the remainder of the
day he scrupulously spent in religious reading,
meditation and prayer. At home or abroad, he
never traveled or visited, wrote letters or trans-
acted any business on the Lord's day; never spent
the day, or any portion of it, in walking, talking,
riding, in any mere recreation or amusement.
When he was all ready to commence his voyage
to Europe, the vessel on which he had engaged
his passage, and expected to sail about the middle
of the week, was detained two or three days by
a violent storm. Sabbath morning the weather
was fair, and the captain, crew and passengers
were all eager and impatient to spread sails. But
Mr. Williston refused to embark on the Lord's
day, although, according to usage, he thereby forfeited his passage money as well as delayed his
passage. The captain, however, at length yielded
to his convictions and convenience; they sailed
Monday morning, and reached Liverpool in advance of all the vessels that sailed from New York
on the previous Sunday. On the same principle,

he chose to be left at a comfortless way station midway over the Alps at midnight Saturday night, rather than to continue his journey on the Sabbath. He reverenced the Sabbath and the sanctuary. He was planted in the house of the Lord, and he flourished in the courts of our God.

If we turn now from this outline of his private, public and religious life to a consideration of some of the chief elements of his character and usefulness, the first question which will spontaneously arise in most minds will be, what was the secret of his success in business.

The secret of what he *did* lay in what he *was*, as is always true, especially of men who do *much*, and the foundation of what he was, was laid, of course, in the nature which God gave him. He inherited from his parents a good physical and mental constitution. He had a healthy body, an attractive person, and a well-balanced mind. In childhood and youth his mind and manners were cultivated in good schools, but still more in the best society; for there is no better society than that which gathers about the fireside of a New England pastor and forms the circle in which he moves. He always mourned his loss of a classical education, and was disposed to depreciate himself

unduly in comparison with educated men. This
felt want of the education of the schools was in-
tensely aggravated in his own view by the early
failure and perpetual weakness of his eye-sight.
Never after he was of age was he able to read
through a book or an article. Never during all
his business and public life could he read his own
correspondence, a newspaper, or even a chapter of
the Bible. But he triumphed over all these ad-
verse circumstances, and wrested wisdom, in spite
of fate, from the very clutches of necessity. Mrs.
Williston read everything to him and for him; the
ear took the place of the eye, oral of written instruction, somewhat as in the primitive ages; he
remembered whatever he heard, and was remark-
ably well informed on all subjects of general and
practical interest. He educated himself by the
discipline of necessity, and the rub and polish of
intelligent work, and the attritions of business, and
association with cultivated men and women, and
observation of men and things, and travel in his
own country and in foreign lands, and faithful improvement of every opportunity for learning and
general culture. Thus he acquired an education that
fitted him better than any mere book knowledge
for the work to which he was called, and qualified

7

him, not indeed to shine in the pulpit, or on the platform, or in the popular assembly (for he was neither born nor trained to be an orator), but to adorn private, social and public life.

A benignant countenance, a commanding and yet winning presence, gentle speech and courteous manners were no unimportant elements of his power and influence. He was a *gentleman*, not only in the parlor and the social circle, but in the office, in the bank, on the street, and in all his business relations. His gentle manners and winning ways attracted strangers, won the hearts of his workmen, and predisposed merchants and manufacturers to transact business with him. He had an eye for beauty. He cultivated a taste for architecture and works of art. As his means enlarged, his style of dress, his manner of living, his house and furniture and grounds were attractive as became a gentleman in his station, and he adorned his native place with public edifices in which utility and beauty were most happily combined.

The habits of economy and industry, in which he was brought up from his childhood, and to which he adhered through all his subsequent life, were among the most obvious and direct means of his prosperity. He never wasted either time

or money. At the summit of his wealth and liberality, he was never above the practice of economy; and with good reason, for economy was the
very foundation both of his wealth and his liberality. Even so our Lord, after feeding thousands
miraculously with a few loaves and fishes, bade his
disciples "Gather up the fragments that remain,
that nothing may be lost." He was always a man
of indefatigable industry. In his early life, he
worked hard with his hands; in middle life and
old age, he worked equally hard with his mind.
Like the celebrated painter, he mixed all his colors
with *brains*. Till he had passed the prime of life,
he used to rise at five and breakfast at six; then
followed the devotions of the family and the closet,
which he never omitted, however great the pres-
sure and hurry of business. Then he would follow his business, or rather *lead* it, all day long,
working as many hours as any day laborer; and
in the evening, he was always busy answering
letters, reading newspapers and useful books, or
rather hearing them read, and devoting to the improvement of his mind, and the acquisition of useful knowledge, every moment that was not due to
domestic, social and religious duty. He was never
too old to learn, and never too rich to be industrious.

This indefatigable industry was accompanied and
made effectual by indomitable perseverance and
unconquerable resolution. He always considered and
reconsidered any new enterprise of importance before he undertook it, weighed it carefully in his
own mind and in his own room, where there was
nothing to disturb his deliberations, consulted others if it was a matter that admitted and required
consultation, and took counsel with God in repeated seasons of prayer. When he had thus decided upon an undertaking, he executed it with
unhesitating promptness and irresistible firmness.
Nothing could then stop him but absolute impos-
sibilities. There was no such word as *can't* in his
vocabulary, but *I will*, or *I'll try*, was on every page
of his dictionary. If the roof of the seminary building blew off in the night, the next morning the
men and the materials were engaged, perchance on
hand, for replacing it. If the church was burned
to the ground, or almost demolished by the fall
of the steeple, nothing was to be done but to rebuild it at once in better style than ever. If a
mill-dam was swept away the first time the water
was let in, and the quicksands rendered it im-
practicable to rebuild it on the same spot, it
could and should be constructed a little higher up

the stream; and it was done at an expense of twenty or thirty thousand dollars; but it brought him hundreds of thousands in the end. These two things, caution and deliberation in deciding, and then promptness and firmness in executing—these two things he was accustomed to consider the main secret of his success in business.

There are two other things which stand in a similar relation to each other, which I cannot but think, were scarcely less conducive to his great prosperity. The first is, that he attended to his own business. He not only oversaw and directed the whole, but he looked with his own eyes into the minutest details. Perhaps he carried this to an unnecessary minuteness that was exhausting to himself and tedious to his factors and agents. I have heard this criticism. But he was fully persuaded that it was essential to success. And Franklin seems to have been of the same opinion:

> He that by the plow would thrive,
> Himself must either hold or drive.

Take care of the pennies and the pounds will take care of themselves. I have no doubt that the constant presence of his eye and his hand was worth thousands of dollars to his business, every year, to

the very last year of his life. The value of that
constant presence and influence not only to his
business, but to the town, to the Seminary, and
even to Amherst College, we can fully appreciate,
like many of our richest blessings, only by its
loss. I am confident we shall all estimate it far
higher ten years hence than we do to-day.

While he was thus watchful and careful in the
supervision of his own affairs, in beautiful equipoise
with this, like those centripetal and centrifugal
forces which preserve the equilibrium of the material universe, he was not less remarkable for the
wisdom and skill with which he selected and employed the agency of others. He had a rare power
of discerning character. He seldom mistook in his
judgment of men. I have myself had a great
deal to do with him in canvassing the merits of
teachers and preachers; and I have always been
struck with his wisdom and discernment. In the
sphere of his own business, his judgment would,
of course, be still more unerring. He always
thought himself *fortunate*—I think he was also wise
—in obtaining the very best men, at once capable
and faithful, for partners, superintendents, agents
and employees of every kind in his business. And
this, in my opinion, was among the main secrets of

his success. It always has been a chief element of power and greatness in the history of great men. It is only a few things, at most, that any man can see directly with his own eyes and do with his own hands. The rest he must accomplish through the agency of other men. He therefore who knows how to find the right men and put them in the right place—as Socrates, that profound thinker and observer of human affairs, has remarked—he it is that accomplishes almost without fail whatever he undertakes.

He not only *found* superior men to co-operate with him, but what was more, what was a striking proof of his own greatness, he developed them, he trained them, he *made* them—made them not merely his agents but his partners and coadjutors, and, like those institutions which he founded, left them to live when he was dead, to work when his work was done, to continue and extend his business, to widen and deepen his influence, to beautify and build up Easthampton, to support and strengthen Payson Church, and, in person and through those whom *they* in like manner shall raise up, to foster and found colleges, seminaries, missions and charitable institutions in this vicinity, in this and in other lands, that shall not only last but live and

do good and bless the church and the world till
time shall be no more.

Besides the wise and good men whom he
thus trained and educated, he had two silent partners that were worth more to him and to his
business than they all. The best partners any man
can have—and every good man *may* have them—
are a prudent, pious, loving wife, and a wise, kind,
guarding and guiding Heavenly Father. The man
who always takes counsel with the unerring intui-
tions and Christian impulses of a good wife, and with
the providence, word and spirit of God, will seldom,
if ever, go astray, and can hardly fail to be a
wise, prosperous, useful and happy man. And
such, I need not say, was the supreme felicity of
Samuel Williston. *He* could meet the challenge
of the wise man in the last chapter of Proverbs
triumphantly, and answer his question without a
moment's hesitation: "Who can find a virtuous
woman? for her price is far above rubies. The
heart of her husband doth safely trust in her, so
that he shall have no need of spoil. She will do
him good and not evil all the days of her life. She
seeketh wool and flax, and worketh willingly with
her hands. She is like the merchants' ships, she
bringeth her food from afar. Her husband is

known in the gates, when he sitteth among the
elders of the land. She maketh fine linen and
selleth it; and delivereth girdles unto the merchants. She openeth her mouth with wisdom, and
in her tongue is the law of kindness. Her children rise up and call her blessed; her husband
also, and he praiseth her. Many daughters have
done virtuously, but thou excellest them all." That
picture does not need to be labeled.

With this accurate knowledge of men, was associated a no less discriminating and correct discernment of things. He kept himself well informed
in matters of business, politics, morals and religion.
He observed, he read, he inquired, he reflected.
And when he acted, it was with such an insight
into the present and such a foresight of the future, that he rarely made a mistake in his judgment of markets, stocks and prices: and business
men who knew him were not afraid to buy when
Mr. Williston bought, and thought it wise to sell
when Mr. Williston sold. The wisdom and success
with which he conducted his large business amid
all the conflicting currents, quicksands and breakers
of peace and war, of commercial changes and political revolutions, till he had reached the age of
three-score years and ten, show a capacity that

8

could have guided the ship of state or the finances
of the nation, if the helm had been committed to
his hands.

With these high intellectual endowments, he
united that integrity and fidelity to all his engagements which alone can inspire confidence, and therefore which alone can ensure lasting prosperity.
Almost at the beginning of his business in the great
cities, he had gained such a character for honesty
and honor, that large merchants would give him a
carte blanche for their orders, and ask no questions
about prices, saying, "You know best—look at our
stock—see what we want, and supply the deficiency."
And this character he never forfeited. All who had
dealings with him knew that he would be faithful to
his engagements, and would expect them to be
prompt in the fulfillment of theirs. Scrupulously
honest and conscientious in the minutest details of
business himself, he acted in strict conformity with
the golden rule, when he required the same minute
exactness of others in business transactions. Thus
he inculcated honesty, while, at the same time, he
inspired confidence, in all around him.

But he was more than conscientious. He aimed to
be Christian in the management of his business.
From the time already mentioned when he renewed

his consecration to the service of God, he regarded
his time and talents and property and business, as no
longer his own. The business was the Lord's, and
he was merely the agent. The Lord was the owner
of the property, and he was only a trustee, an over-
seer, a steward intrusted with the care and management of it. Of course, he felt bound to conduct the
business in accordance with the will of the owner,
to pay over the income at his order, and to hold
the principal subject to his disposal. This, therefore,
he made the matter of his daily, and almost hourly
study, meditation and prayer. No other subject
occasioned him so much thought and anxiety. Besides his regular hours of prayer, morning and evening, he had his special seasons of prayer and self-
examination every week ; he asked wisdom from on
high in ejaculatory petitions many times a day, and
took counsel with God and with wise and good men
at every suitable opportunity, and all with reference
to this more than any, and perhaps all other questions: How shall I best serve God in the use of
the property, and in the conduct of the business
with which he has intrusted me. And when we have
taken into account all the other elements that entered directly and obviously into the result, I cannot
doubt that we must reckon in the special blessing of

Heaven on this method of conducting his business as the grand secret of his prosperity. Such, at any rate, was the light in which he was always in the habit of looking at the subject.

Mr. Williston was not naturally more generous than other men. It was the regenerating, and sanctifying grace of God, that made him such a liberal giver. When, in their poverty, his parents persisted in giving for charitable objects, Samuel, who was toiling on the farm for the support of the family, and who was not then a converted man, sometimes doubted if it were not an excess of charity. More than once I have heard him say that he thought it hard when his father subscribed a few dollars to aid the college to which he has, himself, given hundreds of thousands. He had a natural love of money, and the value which he attached to it was enhanced by the want of it which he experienced in early life, and still further strengthened by the very nature and processes of the business in which the foundations of his fortune were laid. When he began to accumulate rapidly, ambition, of which he was by no means destitute, would most naturally have conspired with the desire of accumulation and impelled him in a bold career of enlarging his business, investing his gains, and thus amassing an immense property. From his own testimony, as well as from the nature of the case and the judgment of others, I am led to believe that it cost him a struggle with his natural inclinations, and his early habits—more of a struggle than it does many men—to distribute his income for charitable objects, instead of investing it for larger, and more rapid accumulation. It was not for his own pleasure or reputation—such was his testimony on the subject—it was not for his own present gratification or future fame that he gave away his thousands, and hundreds of thousands. But, if he knew his own heart, it was from Christian principle; it was from a sense of duty to God and mankind. The love of Christ constrained him, and no other power could have impelled him to such labors, self-denials and sacrifices.

Benevolence was not so much a passion as a principle with Mr. Williston, and he conducted his charities with just as much method and system as he did his business. "Method is the very hinge of business," was the placard which was ever before the eyes of the workmen in his button mill. The same motto governed his whole religious life. He planned his giving on the same magnificent scale, and with the same thoughtful forecast as he

did his manufacturing; adhered to his beneficent
plans, promises and engagements, with the same
fixed purpose; disbursed charities as regularly and
systematically as he paid debts or wages; met
calls for extraordinary donations, as promptly and
liberally, as hopefully and courageously as he did
unforeseen exigencies in his business, and was
as ready to borrow money, if need be, for the one
purpose as for the other. Indeed, his pledges
were almost always in advance of his receipts.
He pledged the money for Williston Seminary,
and for each of his $50,000 donations to Amherst
College, before he had made it, and he often did
the same to meet an emergency of the American
Board and of Home Missions. He would no more
have lost a great opportunity of doing good for
want of money, actually in hand, than he would
for that reason, have let slip a rare chance of making a pecuniary investment. In short, nothing
shows more clearly the consistency and true greatness of his character, than the fact that he was so
manifestly one and the same man, acting on the
same principles, and by the same methods, whether
in his business or his religion. He made a religion of his business, and he made a business of
his religion. They were only different departments

of the same great life-work wherein the business
methodized, informed and vitalized the religion,
while the religion, in turn, elevated, hallowed and
transfigured the business. In this, as in many
other things, he showed himself a genuine son of
the Puritans, though with better manners and in
a happier age. In this he was like Paul and
John; nay, in this he was like Christ.

The aggregate of Mr. Williston's charities, in
his life-time, must have exceeded a million of dollars. His will provides for the distribution of
from one-half to three-quarters of a million more.
Considerably more than half of this magnificent
sum he gave to two institutions. So far from
regretting that he had done so, his only regret
as he drew near to the time when he must give
an account of his stewardship, was, that he could
not do more—that he could not endow the college as richly as he did the seminary, and furnish
it as amply for its great and good work. This
regret — I state it on the very best authority—
this regret weighed on his heart, wore upon his
health, and helped to shorten his life. The sor-
est trial of his later years was, not the loss of
property, not the mortification of comparative
failure in his last business enterprise, but that he

was thereby prevented from providing his beloved Amherst with the pecuniary means of realizing his exalted idea of a Christian college.

Providence had obviously raised him up and marked him out to be a founder of educational institutions His own experience, both positive and negative, his high appreciation of what education he had, and his passionate desire, his long hunger and intense thirst for more, impressed him deeply with the value of the higher education given in academies and colleges. His experience as a charity student at Phillips Academy showed him the necessity of funds and endowments to such institutions. His subsequent prosperity gave him the means of providing such funds. His religious character and experience emphasized to him the unspeakable worth of *Christian* seminaries of learning. His views and feelings and motives in this regard were precisely such as inspired the original founders of Amherst College. He wished to found and foster institutions for the glory of God, and the salvation of men ; for the propagation of truth and righteousness in the earth. He saw that there was room for another and better Phillips Academy, in the valley of the Connecticut. He felt that there

was an imperative demand for another college as
richly endowed as Harvard, but more evangelical,
more Christian, in old Massachusetts. And he
believed that there could be no better location
for such institutions, than old Hampshire, his
native county, which, as statistics showed, already
surpassed all other counties in its percentage of
educated men and of church members. He *believed* in endowing institutions of learning and religion. He had good reason for this; therein as
we have seen, he placed himself among the wisest,
greatest, and most far-seeing of mankind. And
whatever Mr. Williston did, he believed in doing
it well. He always made, and provided for, the
best things of their kind—the best houses, the
best mills, the best machinery, the best fabrics,
the best church edifices, the best colleges and seminaries of learning; believing this to be at once
the truest economy and the wisest policy. Like
the historians and artists of ancient Greece, he
wished his work to endure and be "a possession
forever;" and it is only the *best* structures, those
which *cost* time and money, that endure.

Besides these two great and permanent institutions, however, he was a constant and liberal
giver to a great variety of literary, charitable and

religious objects. He contributed liberally, *very* liberally to the support of the gospel at home. He was an unfailing contributor to the regular periodical charities of the church of which he was a member. His donations to the great national societies, especially for the freedmen and home and foreign missions, were as constant as the seasons, and as generous as his resources were large. He sowed beside all waters, at the same time that he planted trees, and laid foundations for many generations.

Those who are skilled in such calculations can easily calculate what this million of dollars which Mr. Williston distributed in his life-time, would have amounted to at the time of his death, if it had all been invested as fast as it accrued at compound interest; and we all know it would have been a vast sum; it would have made one of the richest men of this age of millionaires. And how easy it would have been for him when he had made, we will say, his first fifty or hundred thousand dollars, instead of expending so much of it for charitable purposes, or even laying it out in the extension of his business, to have invested it all, as fast as it came in, in *stocks* and *bonds* and *mortgages*. But where would Easthampton then have been; where

then would have been Williston Seminary; what
then would have become of Amherst College; and
where would our Missionary Boards and Sanitary
and Christian Commissions have looked for help in
their exigencies? It would have been a luxury
for a selfish miser—it would have been a natural
and an intellectual pleasure for Mr. Williston to
have sat still and seen his property roll up, tens of
thousands, hundreds of thousands, millions, perchance tens of millions, into a more than princely
fortune. But how much purer and sweeter the
pleasure of seeing his native town prosper, and the
Seminary that bears his name grow, and the College
that he saved extending its influence—how much
greater the luxury of employing and supporting
hundreds of families and thousands of hands in his
business, and enlightening the eyes, gladdening the
hearts, saving the souls of a multitude that no man
can number, in this and in other lands, by the
fruits of his beneficence! Mr. Williston had the
wisdom to make this better choice, and the satisfaction of seeing in part its happy results; and I
bless God that we whom he has associated with
himself in some of his counsels and trusts, have
been permitted to rejoice with him in this supreme
satisfaction.

Mr. Williston had an ear for music; he enjoyed highly and intelligently appreciated, as we all know, the performances of the choice bands which he was at so much pains and expense to procure for the Anniversaries of Williston Seminary. But he once said to me that " the hum of the factory was sweeter music than the best concert he ever heard." *There* was a genuine *born business* man. But that was not the whole significance of the remark. In order to understand all the sweetness of that music, the end which he sought in his business must be taken into consideration, as well as the means to that end. There *is* no happiness for man on earth like that of a great and good work prosecuted diligently, enthusiastically, for a *great and good end*. *That* was the music which filled the ear and inspired the soul of Mr. Williston. I pity the man who hath none of this music in him. He is fit for treason, stratagems and spoils.

Mr. Williston was not a mere accumulator of money. He was a creator of values. He was an inventor of new fabrics, and new ways and means for their manufacture. He was an originator of new enterprises. He was the first and for some time the only manufacturer of covered buttons in the country. The manufacture of elastic suspenders

was also a new industry. Most of the other manufactures which he and his partners introduced into
Easthampton were comparatively new enterprises.
He kept in advance of the line of march in trade
and manufactures, and by the time the rest of the
line came up so as to share the business and divide
the profits, he was ready, if necessary, to enter
upon some new and more remunerative business.
At the same time, so far-seeing and so conservative
have been his plans, that the *first* button company
of the country is *now* the largest covered-button
concern in the world; and most of the other com-
panies still take the lead in their several lines of
business. Williston Seminary, founded to be a classical school of the highest order and to become an
English college, was a new idea; or, rather, it was
at once novel and conservative—it was, like the
works of God and all the greatest and best works
of men, a *development* and at the same time a *crea-
tion.* And the way in which he provided in his
will for its continued growth and progress for at
least a generation or two to come, was as unique as
the institution itself, and as sagacious as it was
original and peculiar.

An almost uninterrupted tide of prosperity bore
Mr. Williston along from year to year, and from

one new and successful enterprise to another, for more than thirty years, until in 1866, when he was already more than three-score years and ten, he entered upon by far the largest and most adventurous of all his undertakings; the building of the last Williston mill and the manufacture of cotton sewing thread. This proved a failure, cost him the direct loss of half a million of money, and indirectly no one can calculate how much more, oppressed his declining years with disappointment and anxiety, brought on a torturing, chronic, incurable disease, and shortened his days by perhaps a decade of years that should have been the most fruitful and happy years of his life. His own judgment in review of this period of life is contained in the last letter which I ever received from him, in which he says, " My experience leads me to think that a man of seventy years should draw his business into a smaller compass rather than enlarge it." It is understood that he did not follow the advice of one of his silent partners in this move. Whether he misunderstood the counsel of the other, or whether a kind and wise Providence intended to teach him lessons in the school of adversity that he could never have learned in prosperity, and

to bestow on him inward and spiritual blessings
of far more value than money, is a question
which can be answered only in the light of another world. It is not strange, however, that he
took that unfortunate step. His prosperity was at
the spring-tide. The successes and gains of the
war were enormous. He was flush with health,
strength, courage, hope, self-reliance and trust in
God. Ambition and benevolence both seemed to
bid him go forward. That music which so charmed
and inspired him at once as a business man and
a Christian, filled his ears and impelled him on-
ward. So far as success in business was con-
cerned, it was now destined to prove the song of
the sirens. But it had been the song of the seraphs
in all his previous life, and how was he to dis-
tinguish? But, perhaps, this sore trial was needful for his spiritual good. Doubtless, on the whole,
it was wisely ordered, and sanctified and over-
ruled to work in him the peaceable fruits of
righteousness. Certainly he developed under its
influence in his latter days some of the sweetest,
loveliest, richest fruits of his broad, deep and man-
ifold character.

He has been accused, perhaps I should say sus-
pected, of being ambitious and of giving, not so

much for the sake of alleviating sorrow and doing
good, as of gaining a name. But what great and
good man is not ambitious? If it is a weakness,
it is the last infirmity of noble minds. When
wisely guided and properly controlled, it is the
strongest and grandest impulse to great achieve-
ments. A sanctified ambition is one of the holi-
est motives to good works. And who does not
aspire to a good name? Has not inspiration pro-
nounced it to be better than precious ointment?
In due subordination to other and higher principles, the desire to perpetuate one's name is a
proper motive for a man and a Christian. And
if ever a man fully resolved and strove earnestly
to keep this motive in complete subordination to
the glory of God and the good of mankind, that
man—if I knew him, and if he knew himself—
that man was Mr. Williston. When a great object was to be accomplished, he was as willing to
give large sums of money without his name as
with it. Witness his munificent donation to Walker
Hall in Amherst, which was to bear the name of
another donor, and his repeated efforts to obtain
still larger donations both from Dr. Walker and
Mr. Hitchcock, whom a selfish ambition would
rather have discouraged and set aside as rivals, as

competitors for the highest place among the friends
and patrons of the institution. It was not merely
to perpetuate his own memory that he gave his
name to the seminary, and the foundations which
he established. It was essential to the prosperity
and usefulness of Williston Seminary that it should
be called, not like high schools and small academies,
by the name of the place, but like other larger and
better endowed institutions, by the name of the
founder; and for this reason, he was *urged* by his
wisest and best counselors, to give it his name. It
was for the interest of Amherst College that his
foundations and his college edifice, should be called
by his name, as an advertisement to the public,
that it was at least, partially endowed, and also as
an example and an inducement to others to do
likewise. And if the Trustees should vote to call
the *institution* "Williston College, or the University
at Amherst," as he forbade them to do while he
lived, but as in gratitude and honor they are bound
to do, now that he is dead, and as every officer and
every student who was connected with it, when he
made the donation that saved it, would hold up both
hands to have them do, it would not redound more
to the honor of the donor, than it would conduce
to the reputation and prosperity of the institution.

10

He has been charged with driving sharp bargains, getting a great deal of work out of his men, and too rigidly exacting every cent of his dues. It is a charge which is often made against those who have grown rich by close calculations, careful watching of the markets and nice balancing of wages and prices, especially in the manufacture and sale of small articles at an almost infinitesimally small profit on each article. Sometimes it is made honestly and candidly, but frequently, I suspect, in sheer envy and jealousy; and generally, I think, it is made ignorantly, without any real consideration of the facts or the principles involved. The same charge was made against Samuel Budgett, the Christian merchant and philanthropist of Kingswood, near Bristol, England, who began his career of money-making and money-saving in his boyhood, when he picked up a horseshoe, went three miles with it and got a penny for it, and continued it till he gave away $10,000 a year for philanthropic objects. And the charge was answered at length, and I think conclusively, by Mr. Bayne in his "Christian Life." The chief points of his answer are briefly these: To buy cheap and sell dear is the law of trade and the only way fortunes are made. In this process he

who has the capital and the faculty will inevitably
have the advantage over him who has not. It
you see the gleam of a gold vein where I saw
only clay, the reward is justly yours; if you know
the ground where corn will grow better than I,
your sheaves must be more numerous than mine;
if you have stronger sinews and more perseverance, and choose to toil for hours in the wester-
ing sun after I have unyoked my team, you must
lay a wider field under seed than I. The pearls
are for him that can and will dive, the golden
apples for him that can and will climb. His men
had a profound knowledge that he was not to be
trifled with. The incompetent and the indolent
were promptly discharged. A man must perform
what he undertook, or he must go. "Why, sir,"
said one who had been long in his service, "I do
believe as *he* would get, ay, just twice as much
work out o' a man in a week as another master."
Business is one thing and charity is another.
Business must be conducted in business ways and
on business principles. Now, large gains by means
of small profits on large sales is a prime rule, is
almost a first principle of success in trade or manufactures. And to demand that this shall be given
up in one instance—whether it be by increase of

wages, reduction of prices, relaxation of services or release of debts, is virtually to demand that it shall be given up in all cases; and to give it up in all cases were to knock out the very corner-stone both of individual success and of public prosperity. All that can be demanded under the name of manufacturing or mercantile honor is, not charity, but justice and fairness. And this, not charity, but justice and fairness, is at once for the individual weal and for the public good. It is nature's own way of spurring on the indolent and having her work well done; and however individuals may smart or grumble, it most effectually subserves the interests of the community.

He sometimes gave offence to employees by the rare truthfulness and frankness with which he told them what was for their good. He never feared to speak out what he believed to be his own rights, or their duties in the relation that existed between them. He never would conceal or disguise the truth when, in his opinion, justice to himself or the welfare of others required it to be spoken. Severe in judging himself, he sometimes became conscious that he had been too severe in censuring others, and then he was just as frank in retracting the censure as he had been in

uttering it, and just as ready to make honorable
amends to the humblest workman as he would
have been to a person of the most exalted station.

He not only condescended to men of low estate,
but when time permitted, and as occasion required,
he conversed with them in the most intimate and
winning way. He sympathized with the poor, for
he had been poor, and he proved himself to them
a friend in need and so a friend indeed. For he not
only gave them money, which is a comparatively
easy thing for a man of wealth to do, but what is
far better, he gave them thought and care and
wise counsel; he tried to put them in the way
of earning a livelihood for themselves; he helped
them to form habits of industry, economy, temperance and piety; he suffered with them in their
sorrows and rejoiced with them in their prosperity;
he was always faithful and true to them, though
they did not always fulfill their promises to him;
in short, he was a father to them, and like their
Father in Heaven, he was kind even to the un-
thankful and the evil. I have in my possession
the strongest written testimonies to this effect,
accompanied by the most touching expressions of
gratitude and affection from those whom he thus
befriended in health and in sickness, and whom

he thus lifted from extreme poverty to circumstances of comparative comfort and independence.

Mr. Williston's character was not perfect, any
more than his judgment was infallible. Doubtless
he had much to contend with. Great men, strong
natures always have. But who of us *is* perfect. He
that is without sin among you, let him cast the first
stone. And when we look at the pure, solid, mas-
sive gold of his noble character and his useful life,
the canker and rust of real faults is scarcely dis-
cernible; while some of these alleged faults are
seen to be only the alloy which is essential to the
value and use of the current coin.

The history of Mr. Williston's private life was
quite peculiar. His domestic and social affections
were tender and strong. When he had already
come to be a prosperous and, for those times, a
wealthy man, a friend congratulated him on his success in business. His reply was, " I would gladly
give up every dollar and begin life a poor man, if I
could only have back my children that I have lost."
If we may trust the testimony of their grandmother
Williston—a partial, perhaps, and yet a competent
and credible witness—they were singularly lovely
and beautiful children, constitutionally, if not even
morbidly, gentle, amiable and religious, such chil-

dren, "with less of earth in them than heaven,"
as give us glimpses of what the children of God
are in their Father's house, and so, as "fire ascend-
ing seeks the sun," they were soon translated to
their proper sphere. Ere this, we may believe,
they have been restored to the embrace of their
loving, longing father. Perhaps they were wait-
ing to welcome him at the heavenly gates, the
same yet how different, still childlike and distinctly recognizable, yet in what loftier stature and
in such forms of seraphic beauty and glory as we
can scarcely imagine.

He loved also his adopted children, cherished
them in their childhood, cared for their education,
rejoiced in their ripening virtues and graces, and
felt, as well he might, all a father's complacency in
their character, pleasure in their prosperity, pride
and exultation in their honors and successes. And
when at the celebration of their golden wedding,
their eight children (counting husbands and wives)
and their sixteen grandchildren were gathered about
them at the old homestead, it was as pretty a picture as is often seen in this imperfect world; nothing
seemed wanting to make their happiness complete.

And that husband and wife, during the fifty-two
years that they were spared to each other, how

had they shared each other's toils and cares, consulted each other's interests and wishes, and known
each other's inmost thoughts and feelings as if they
were their own; how had they planned and prayed
and sorrowed and rejoiced together; how had they
always traveled together and returned together,
visited or staid at home together, gone out and
come in and risen up and sat down together, and
lived and moved and had their being in and for
each other, always not only one flesh, but palpably
one mind, one heart, one spirit—*almost always in
one place*, till they seemed, even to their neighbors, how much more to themselves, inseparable
the one from the other! She was eyes and ears
and feet and hands to him. He was head and
heart and soul and spirit to her. Each was the
other's life—each the other's higher, better, dearer
self. Who can conceive the pang, the *wrench* when
such a couple are separated — who imagine the
blessedness of a speedy, perfect and perpetual re-
union in heaven!

Mr. Williston's relation to his brothers was beautiful; his affection for them was very tender. Samuel
resembled his mother; Nathan is the living image
of his father; Payson was like and yet strangely
unlike both. And it seemed as if the spirits of

the parents hovered over the brothers whenever
they met, and drew them towards each other with
a more than fraternal love. The two brothers who
have deceased were as unlike each other in their
person, manners and character as they were in
their ways of doing good—the one ever sowing
seed for an immediate harvest, the other planting
trees and founding institutions for many generations.
It was beautiful to hear them rally each other on
their differences and their peculiarities, and at the
same time to see how manifestly they sought the
same end in different ways, and, although person-
ally unlike, they were one in spirit. Lovely and
pleasant in their lives, in death they were not
long divided. But, methinks, the happiness of the
two brothers will not be quite perfect till the third
has joined them in the better land.

Mr. Williston had a healthy and hearty affection
for his native place. I fear his fellow-townsmen
do not realize how much he loved it, nor fully appreciate how much he has done for it. I suspect
they do not know, as well as I do, how near they
came to losing him. He believed he might become
richer, he hesitated for a time whether he might
not also be more useful, to found Williston Seminary somewhere else, and himself go with it. After

11

much prayerful and anxious deliberation, he decided
to remain; and love for the place of his birth was
one, and not the smallest, of the weights that turned
the scale. He found Easthampton a mere hamlet,
with an old meeting-house on the common and a
few poor farms scattered around. He left it one
of the richest and most beautiful towns in Hampshire County, a great educational and manufacturing
center, with beautiful farm-houses, (villas they might
almost be called,) and several model villages clus-
tering about elegant churches and a model seminary of learning. He turned its very brooks into
silver and its sands to gold—not, however, the gold
and silver of the miser, but that of the Latin
poet, which shines only by its *use*. The town
will be known in history as his birthplace.
Strangers will visit the spot where he was born,
the house in which he lived and died, and the grave
in which he was buried—*he* who founded Williston
Seminary, and saved Amherst College, and lived
and acquired wealth only to glorify God and do
good to men. And not only the seminary, but the
town, will be the monument of Samuel Williston.

Religion was the controlling principle of Mr.
Williston's life. The editor of the daily morning
newspaper of our valley speaks of the objects of

his life as two: "The making of money and the
serving of God." That is not, perhaps, wide of
the mark. But he himself, I am sure, would have
preferred another way of stating it. In his own
consciousness his object was one, viz., the serving
of God by the making of money. That which
the London Times said of Mr. Peabody may with
equal truth and emphasis be said of Mr. Williston: "He did not become charitable because he
had become rich, but he became rich that he might
be charitable." But with the former charity was
an end, while with the latter even charity was
chiefly a means to please and honor God. Charity
with him was the fruit of Christian piety. Hu-
mility, reverence, worship and obedience were also
marked characteristics of his religion. He *feared*
God and kept his commandments. He was emi-
nently conscientious. He was anxious—literally
and emphatically *anxious,* to know and do his whole
duty. He was inflexibly resolved on doing right.
His theology was that of the Puritans and the Pil-
grim fathers. Like them his religion was cast in
the mould of the Old Testament. The faith, hope,
love and joy of the gospel were not wanting, but
they were less conspicuous. Yet he believed in
the Lord Jesus Christ with all his heart and loved

him supremely. He never doubted the truth of
Christianity, the inspiration of the Scriptures, the
doctrines of evangelical religion, the divinity of
Christ and his power to save the chief of sinners.
He only doubted his own personal relations to
Christ and the great salvation, or as he would have
expressed it, his personal acceptance. Of this he
wanted assurance. This, however, seems to have
been given him, in good measure, as he drew
near his end. "I think I am going through safe—
indeed, I think I may say, I *know* I am." "If there
is anything I hate it is sin; and I *know* I love the
Lord Jesus Christ and his cause." "I am in my
heavenly Father's hands, and he will do that which
is right and best for me." These were among his
last utterances.

He died Saturday, July 18th, and was buried Monday, July 20th, from his own house, which was
filled with the friends and distinguished strangers,
while the people of the town crowded the lawn,
at the doors and beneath the windows, mourners
all, to express their sympathy with the family, to
bemoan their own loss and to do honor to his
memory.

The richest legacy he has left us is his character and his example. Happy will it be for his

family and friends, his neighbors and acquaint-
ances, if they tread in the footsteps of his faith
and good works. It behooves the trustees of the
institutions which he has founded to be faithful
to their trust and keep and build them up on the
foundations which he has laid. He loved them
as his children and provided for them as his heirs;
it is our duty and privilege to care for them as
wards and to cherish them as if they were our
own daughters. The teachers and pupils of these
seminaries should never forget his answer—so often
repeated by his lips and so well illustrated in his
whole life—to the first question in religion and
the highest question in philosophy: What is the
chief end of man? He believed with all his heart
that his chief end and the chief end of *every* man
is "to glorify God and enjoy him forever." He
has taught the rich the right use of money and
the wisdom of being their own executors. And
we may all learn from him the beauty and the
secret of a truly noble life.

www.ingramcontent.com/pod-product-compliance
Lightning Source LLC
Chambersburg PA
CBHW031447270326
41930CB00007B/907